Then and Now

Life at School

Vicki Yates

Heinemann
LIBRARY
Chicago, Illinois

© 2008 Heinemann Library
a division of Reed Elsevier Inc.
Chicago, Illinois

Customer Service 888-454-2279
Visit our website at www.heinemannraintree.com

Designed by Victoria Bevan and Joanna Hinton-Malivoire
Photo research by Ruth Smith and Q2A Solutions
Printed and bound in China by South China Printing Co. Ltd.

12 11 10 09 08
10 9 8 7 6 5 4 3 2 1

ISBN-10: 1-4034-9835-0 (hc)   1-4034-9843-1 (pb)

The Library of Congress has cataloged the first edition of this book as follows:

Yates, Vicki.
  Life at school / Vicki Yates.
     p. cm. -- (Then and now)
  Includes bibliographical references and index.
  ISBN-13: 978-1-4034-9835-9 (hc)
  ISBN-13: 978-1-4034-9843-4 (pb)
  1. Schools--History--Juvenile literature. 2. Students--History--Juvenile literature. I. Title.
  LA11.Y38 2008
  371.009--dc22
                                2007014733

Acknowledgements
The publishers would like to thank the following for permission to reproduce photographs: Alamy pp. **14**, **23** (D. Hurst), **17**
(Sally and Richard Greenhill), **20** (Popperfoto); Bonniej p.**11** (Dreamstime.com); Corbis pp. **6** (H. Armstrong Roberts), **9** (Will
& Deni McIntyre), **22** (Bettmann); Flickr p. **19** (Glenn Loos-Austin); Greater Manchester County Record Office p. **10**, **18**; Library
of Congress p. **8**; New York Picture Library p. **16**; Ottmar Bierwagen p. **7** (photographersdirect.com); Photolibrary.com pp. **5**
(Photo Researchers, Inc), **12** (Nonstock Inc), **13** (Index Stock Imagery); SuperStock p. **21**.

Cover photograph of slate reproduced with permission of Corbis (Tetra Images) and photograph of computer reproduced with
permission of Alamy/archivberlin Fotoagentur GmbH. Back cover photograph reproduced with permission of Alamy/D. Hurst.

Contents

What Is School?

School is where we go to learn.

Most children go to school.

Getting to School

Long ago children walked to school.

Today many children ride buses
to school.

In and Around School

Long ago schools were small.

Today many schools are big.

Long ago classrooms were cold and dark.

Today classrooms are warm
and light.

Learning

Long ago children learned a few subjects at school.

Today we learn many subjects at school.

Long ago children wrote on slate boards.

Today we can write with computers.

Long ago schools had few books.

Today schools can have
many books.

Long ago children exercised at school.

Today children still exercise
at school.

Let's Compare

Long ago school was very different.

How is school different today?

What Is It?

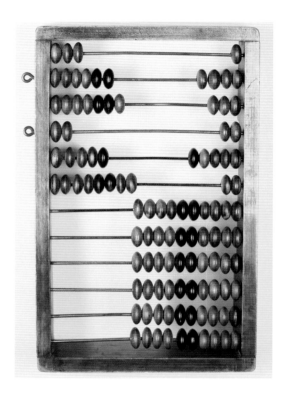

Long ago this object was used in schools. Do you know what it is?

Answer on p. 24

Picture Glossary

slate board a board made from a flat rock called slate. People write on slate boards.

Index

Answer to question on p. 22: It is an abacus. Children used it to help them add and subtract.

Note to Parents and Teachers

Before reading: Ask children why they come to school. Write their ideas on a sheet of paper. Ask them what they like doing best at school. Explain that schools have changed since you went to school. Encourage them to ask you questions about your school days.

After reading: Have children look through the pictures in the book that show the past. Ask them if they notice any other ways school may have been different than it is now.

You can support children's nonfiction literacy skills by helping them use the table of contents, headings, picture glossary, and index.